It wasn't always fun staying at home but we have found ways to make it super fun. When we found out that we had to stay home due to a new virus that's affecting the whole world we were very sad and frustrated.

You mean *I can't go to the movies!*

Mom came up with an idea about movie night and got the popcorn popping, brought out our sleeping bags. The room was cozy and we enjoyed watching so many movies almost as if we were in the movie theater.

Ola and I started to make a list and thought how exciting it was to come up with different ideas.

The next morning I came up with an idea for camping in the backyard. Daddy set up a tent for us. Mommy baked some delicious treats and made some hot cocoa. It was a nice little set up. We enjoyed our treats, marshmallows and cocoa over nice conversations and games.

**Next was gardening, Ola chose a vegetable for us to plant. Mom got us some gardening tools. It was so much fun planting tomato seeds. Mom taught us how to water the plants without over drowning it.
I didn't know plants could drown.**

We couldn't believe our eyes when our vegetables started to grow. We made sure to continue to water our plants and sometimes we even whispered to them a bit. We were officially gardeners and our garden became our pride and Joy day in, day out.

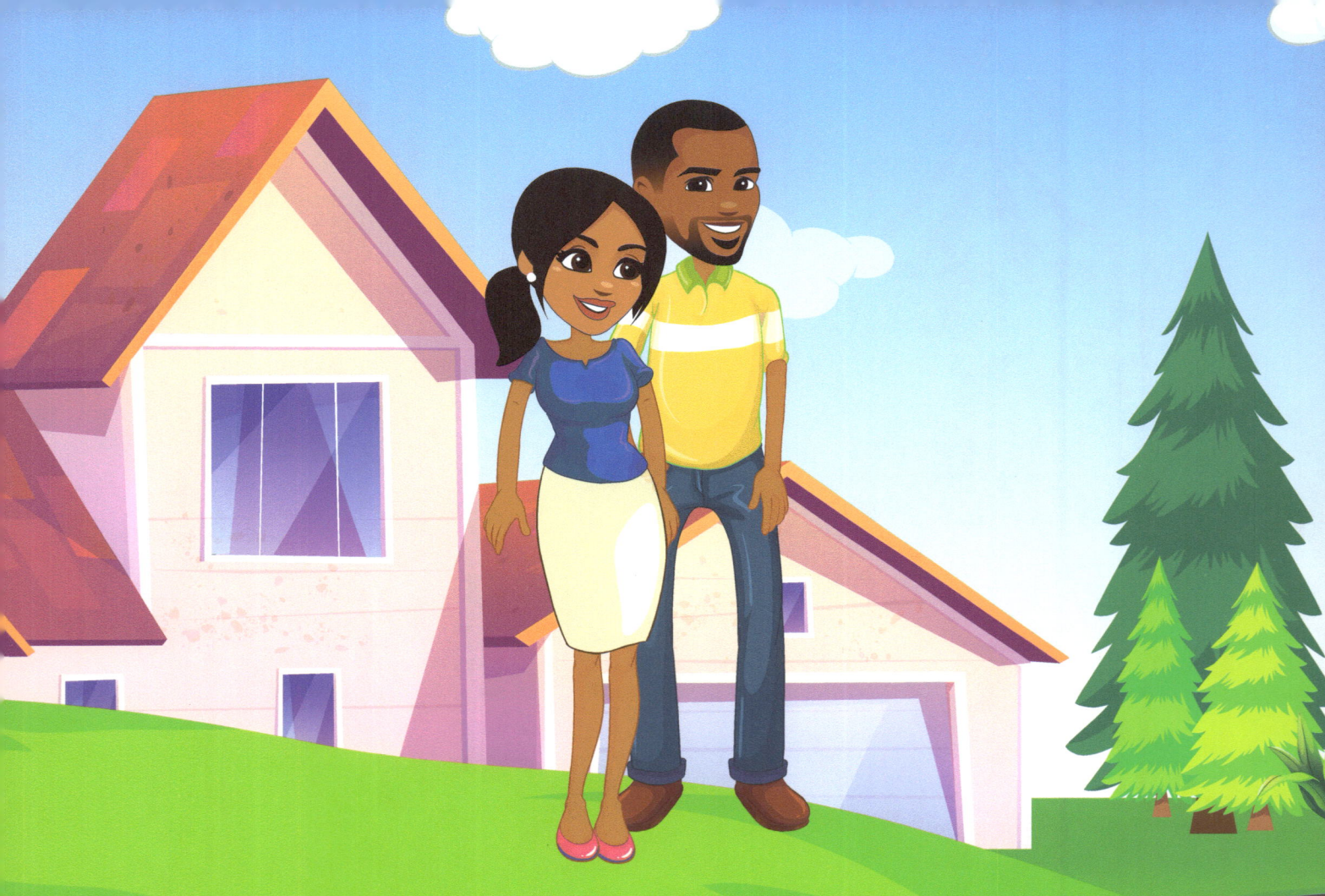

I shouted with amazement! as Ola shouted sliding down the water slide. She smiled so hard her back teeth were showing. She loves water parks! We were so full of ideas for home adventures that our list became more and more. From scavenger hunts to Paintball birthday parties. 3 months have gone by and we almost forgot about all the things we were missing from staying home.

Family time became more and more fun and we became grateful staying home with our family.

www.ingramcontent.com/pod-product-compliance
Lightning Source LLC
Chambersburg PA
CBHW051839210526
45473CB00005B/1942